Learning to Get Along®

Talk and Work It Out

Cheri J. Meiners, M.Ed.
Illustrated by Meredith Johnson

free spirit
PUBLiSHiNG®

Helping kids
help themselves®
since 1983

Library of Congress Cataloging-in-Publication Data
Meiners, Cheri J., 1957–
    Talk and work it out / Cheri J. Meiners ; illustrated by Meredith Johnson.
        p. cm. — (Learning to get along)
    ISBN 1-57542-176-3
1. Interpersonal conflict—Juvenile literature. I. Johnson, Meredith, ill. II. Title. III. Series: Meiners, Cheri J., 1957– . Learning to get along.
    BF637.I48M45 2005
    158.2—dc22

                                                                                        2005000065

Cover and interior design by Marieka Heinlen
Edited by Marjorie Lisovskis

10 9 8 7 6 5 4
Printed in Hong Kong

Free Spirit Publishing Inc.
217 Fifth Avenue North, Suite 200
Minneapolis, MN 55401-1299
(612) 338-2068
help4kids@freespirit.com
www.freespirit.com

Dedication

To my nieces and nephews:
Kris, Katie, Laura, James, Nevin,
Emily, Julie, and Christine
who choose to work
out problems
peacefully

Acknowledgments

I wish to thank Meredith Johnson, whose charming illustrations resonate so well with the text, and Marieka Heinlen for the exuberant design. I appreciate Judy Galbraith and the entire Free Spirit family for their dedicated support of the series. I am especially grateful to Margie Lisovskis for her diplomatic style as well as her talented editing. I also recognize Mary Jane Weiss, Ph.D., for her expertise and gift in teaching social skills. Lastly, I thank my fantastic family—David, Kara, Erika, James, Daniel, Julia, and Andrea—who are each an inspiration to me.

I'm learning to get along
with lots of people.

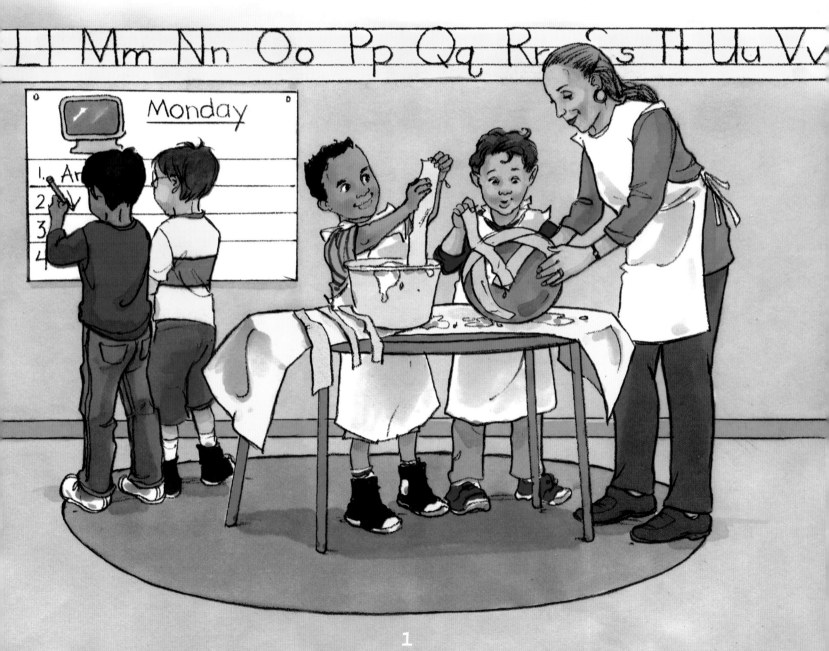

Sometimes I don't agree with a person.

It's okay to have different ideas.

But if something really bothers me,

I can choose to work things out.

I can stop and take a big breath to calm myself.

I can take time to think about what to do.

I may want to talk about the problem.

I can look at the person, and speak up when I tell how I feel.

Talk it out

1. Talk about the problem.
2. Listen to understand.
3. Think of ways to solve it.
4. Choose the best plan.

I can listen and think about
how the other person feels.

I learn more about the problem
when I listen to another view.

I can say back what I hear.

This shows that I understand and care.

As we talk about the problem,
I can be polite and friendly.

It feels good to be heard,
and to understand things better.

I can use my imagination
to help solve the problem.

I can think of lots of ideas.

And I can ask the person to help find an answer.

If I still need help, I can ask a grown-up.

I can think about each idea.

I can help choose a plan that's good for both of us.

I can cooperate to make things work.

I might share, or take turns, or do something nice.

Sometimes it's hard to find an answer everyone likes.

I can still show respect.

I'm learning to solve my problems peacefully.

Getting along can be more important than getting everything I want.

If I care about someone else's ideas and feelings as much as my own,

we can usually find a way
to work things out.

Ways to Reinforce the Ideas in *Talk and Work It Out*

As you read each page spread, ask children:

- What's happening in this picture?

Here are additional questions you might discuss:

Pages 1–5

- Is there someone you often get along with? Why do you enjoy being together? What do you enjoy doing?
- How do you feel when something really bothers you? Whose feelings are you thinking about? Why is it a good idea to try to work things out?

Pages 6–9

- Let's take a slow, big breath. *(Demonstrate inhaling and exhaling slowly. Have children imitate you as you breathe with them.)* How do you feel after taking a deep breath?
- What are some other ways to calm down? *(Discuss strategies such as counting to ten, taking a walk, drawing how you feel, telling a doll or pet about it, talking to an adult, and other ideas children suggest.)*
- To work out a problem with someone, what's the first thing you need to do? *(Calmly tell how you feel.)*
- Will it help most to tell how *you* feel, or to tell the other person what *she* or *he* did wrong? Why?
- When you talk to someone, where do you look? How loud should your voice be? *(Help children recognize that it's important to look at the other person and to speak up in a calm, steady voice. The goal is to help the person understand without yelling or blaming.)*

Pages 10–15

- What can you do to be a good listener? *(Stay quiet while someone talks, look at the speaker, think about what you hear, say back what you hear, ask questions, and think about the person's feelings.)*
- How do you feel when someone listens to you? How can listening to the other person help solve the problem?

Pages 16–21

- What are some ideas this boy thought of for solving the problem? What other ideas might work?
- How do you think the girl might feel when he asks her for her ideas?
- Who are some grown-ups you can ask for help to solve a problem?

Pages 22–25

- How do you know if something is a good idea? *(Both people will like the idea, it will solve the problem for a long time, no one will get hurt.)*
- What does it mean to cooperate? How are these children cooperating?

Pages 26–29

- When is it hard to find an answer everyone likes?
- What is respect? *(When you show respect to people, you show that you think they are important.)*

- How can you show respect even if you don't agree with someone? *(Stay calm, listen politely, show that you understand how the person feels.)*
- Have you ever tried to make someone else feel happy by doing what the person wanted instead of what you wanted to do? What happened? How did the person feel? How did you feel?

Pages 30–31
- If you care about how someone else feels, how will you act?
- When there's a problem, what can you do to try to work it out? *(You may want to review the steps cited on pages 9 and 33–34 and covered in detail on pages 8–25: Talk about the problem together respectfully, listen, think of possible solutions, choose the best idea to try.)*

Problem-Solving Games

Talk and Work It Out teaches skills for peaceful problem solving. Here is a rhyme that presents the skills in an easy-to-remember four-step model:

1. **Talk about the problem.**
2. **Listen to understand.**
3. **Think of ways to solve it.**
4. **Choose the best plan.**

Read this book often with your child or group of children. Once children are familiar with the book, refer to it when teachable moments arise involving positive behavior and problems related to solving conflicts. Notice and comment when children express their feelings calmly and respectfully, listen to another viewpoint, and work cooperatively to find solutions. In addition, use the following activities to reinforce children's understanding of and facility with skills for resolving problems.

Problem-Solving Finger Play *(reinforces Skill Steps 1–4)*

Have children recite the four problem-solving steps (above) as a poem. Use gestures for the first word in each line: "Talk . . ." (point to your mouth); "Listen . . ." (point to your ear); "Think . . ." (point to your head); "Choose . . ." (point to the palm of your other upheld hand).

I-Messages *(reinforces Skill Step 1)*

Preparation: On index cards, write problem scenarios similar to the following. Use real situations that fit your setting and children, but do not use their real names. On the back of each card, give two example responses. Make the first response an I-message—an assertive, effective response that begins with the word "I" and explains what the child thinks or feels. Make the second response an ineffective one that blames others. Place the cards in a bag.

Sample Scenarios and Responses:
- Someone takes a toy you are playing with. *("I'm still playing with that." "You always take my stuff! Give it back!")*
- Someone calls you a name. *("I don't like being called that." "You are that, too!")*
- One friend lets another friend cut in line ahead of you. *("I was already here. I don't think it's fair to let someone else in." "Hey, you can't do that!")*

Directions: Have a child draw a card. Read the scenario aloud, and then read the responses on the back. Ask, "What's a good way to talk about the problem?" or, "Which one tells how you would feel?" The child chooses the best response. Follow up by asking, "Why is that a good thing to say?" Talk about why a mean or angry "you-message" doesn't help solve a problem. (It blames someone; you and the other person might get more upset; it isn't respectful.) Also talk about how using an I-message can help keep things calm and help everyone stay respectful.

Extension: Have the child suggest a helpful response on his or her own, without the prompts on the back of the card. Then invite children to role-play the scenario.

"Say It Back" Circle Game *(reinforces Skill Step 2)*

Preparation: Have children sit in a circle. For large groups, have more than one circle of 6–8 children. Each circle needs one beanbag or soft toy.

Directions: Name a topic, such as colors (sports, desserts, TV shows, toys, books). Give the beanbag to a child and ask the child to name his or her favorite color. ("I like green.") The child then tosses the beanbag to another child, who "says it back" and then adds a new comment. ("Kayla, you like green. I like purple.") That child then throws the beanbag to another child, and play continues. ("Howie, you like purple. I like pink.") Change the topics randomly. Discuss how well children are listening when they say back what they hear. Also emphasize that although they like different things, they can share their feelings and get along.

Listening with an Open Mind *(reinforces Skill Step 2)*

Materials: Quart-size glass jar with lid, drawing paper and marker, tape, 8–10 clothespins

Preparation: Draw and cut out a face (about 4" high x 3" wide); tape the face to the jar.

Directions: Show children the open jar and say, "Let's pretend this jar is a person." Point to the face: "See—it's the person's head." Put the lid on the jar and say, "When someone won't listen to new ideas, we say the person's mind is closed. Pretend these clothespins are new ideas. Do you think the ideas will go in when the person isn't listening?" After the children guess, stand the jar on the ground with the lid still closed and try to drop clothespins into it. Ask, "What happens to new ideas when we're not listening?" (The ideas don't go in.) Then remove the lid and drop the clothespins again, carefully, so they go into the jar. Say, "When we decide to really listen, we have an open mind. Then we can hear and understand new ideas." Ask, "What can we do to listen with an open mind?" Discuss guidelines such as the following:

- Stay quiet while someone else talks.
- Think about what the person said.
- Ask questions to make sure you understand.
- Look at the person talking.
- Say back what you heard.
- Think about how the person might feel.

Then let children take turns trying to drop clothespins into the jar. When a child's clothespin goes in, ask the child to state a listening guideline.

Variation: Have each child make an individual "open mind" by putting a face on a baby-food jar and dropping in paper clips.

Brainstorming *(reinforces Skill Step 3)*

On index cards, write problem situations that occur in your setting or that you know children will relate to. (See samples, below.) Read or have children read a scenario. Write it at the top of a whiteboard or piece of chart paper. Then say, "Let's *brainstorm* ideas for solving this problem. We'll think of all the things you could possibly do. All ideas are okay when we brainstorm." Prompt children as needed so you have four possible solutions. List the solutions on the board or chart paper. Encourage children to wait to evaluate the ideas until later. You might say, "Later we'll get a chance to choose the best plan. Right now we'll just think of ideas."

After brainstorming, save the whiteboard or chart paper to be used in the following game. Or, if you wish, record all the ideas on the backs of the index cards for future reference.

Sample Problem Scenarios:	**Sample Solutions:**
Someone pushes you in line.	Push the person back. Tell an adult. Say, "I don't like to be pushed." Ignore it.
You and another child want to watch different TV shows.	Turn off the TV. Take turns watching a show. Yell and hit the person. Find a show you both like.

"Choosing the Best Plan" Game and Role Play *(reinforces Skill Step 4)*

Preparation: You will need the problem scenarios and solutions from the "Brainstorming" game. Each child will need paper, a pencil, a blue crayon, and a red crayon.

Level 1

Give children paper and pencils and have them number their paper 1–4. Distribute the red and blue crayons. Read aloud a scenario and the first solution. Ask, "Would this work well for both people? Why or why not?" If the answer is yes, have children draw a red smiley face or star next to number 1. Then ask, "Would this solve the problem for a long time?" If yes, have children draw a blue face or star next to the same number. Continue for each solution. Then ask each child, "Which do you think is the best plan? Why?" Accept all appropriate answers, helping children to understand that the best plan is one that works for both people and can work for a long time.

Level 2

Group children in pairs. Have partners role-play the problem scenario, with one child suggesting the solution she or he chose in Level 1. Then have children switch roles.

Level 3

When a real problem arises, discuss it with the children involved once they are calm. Talk about how they chose to handle the situation, what other options they had, and how they might handle it next time. Children may want to use the system of evaluating solutions with the red and blue crayons to help them in their decision making.

Free Spirit's Learning to Get Along® Series

Help children learn, understand, and practice basic social and emotional skills. Real-life situations, diversity, and concrete examples make these read-aloud books appropriate for childcare settings, schools, and the home. *Each book: $10.95, 40 pp., color illust., S/C, 9" x 9", ages 4–8.*

ACCEPT AND VALUE EACH PERSON
Introduces diversity and related concepts: respecting differences, being inclusive, and appreciating people just the way they are.

REACH OUT AND GIVE
Begins with the concept of gratitude; shows children contributing to their community in simple yet meaningful ways.

SHARE AND TAKE TURNS
Gives reasons to share; describes four ways to share; points out that children can also share their knowledge, creativity, and time.

TALK AND WORK IT OUT
Peaceful conflict resolution is simplified so children can learn to calm down, state the problem, listen, and think of and try solutions.

UNDERSTAND AND CARE
Builds empathy in children; guides them to show they care by listening to others and respecting their feelings.

LISTEN AND LEARN
Introduces and explains what listening means, why it's important to listen, and how to listen well.

BE CAREFUL AND STAY SAFE
Teaches children how to avoid potential dangers, ask for help, follow directions, use things carefully, and plan ahead.

BE POLITE AND KIND
Introduces children to good manners and gracious behavior including saying "Please," "Thank you," "Excuse me," and "I'm sorry."

TRY AND STICK WITH IT
Introduces children to flexibility, stick-to-it-iveness (perseverance), and the benefits of trying something new.

KNOW AND FOLLOW RULES
Shows children that following rules can help us stay safe, learn, be fair, get along, and instill a positive sense of pride.

RESPECT AND TAKE CARE OF THINGS
Children learn to put things where they belong and ask permission to use things. Teaches simple environmental awareness.

WHEN I FEEL AFRAID
Helps children understand their fears; teaches simple coping skills; encourages children to talk with trusted adults about their fears.

JOIN IN AND PLAY
Teaches the basics of cooperation, getting along, making friends, and being a friend.

BE HONEST AND TELL THE TRUTH
Children learn that being honest in words and actions builds self-confidence and trust, and that telling the truth can take courage and tact.

free spirit PUBLISHING®

217 Fifth Avenue North, Suite 200
Minneapolis, MN 55401
toll-free 800.735.7323
local 612.338.2068
fax 612.337.5050
help4kids@freespirit.com
www.freespirit.com